We’ [illegible] g nificent and supposedly indestructible ocean liner sailed from Southampton, England, on April 10, 1912. Several days later, other ships in the area repeatedly wired the *Titanic*, warning of icebergs. The *Titanic* captain and crew ignored the warnings. They were cruising in the greatest ocean liner ever built!

We all know the rest of the story. Shortly before midnight on April 14, the *Titanic* plowed into a huge iceberg, and within hours it sank, claiming over 1,500 lives. This tragedy could have been avoided if the captain and crew had put aside their overconfidence, paid attention to the warnings, and made the necessary adjustments.

Our lenten journey can be like an ocean cruise. You may encounter rough swells of hassles and heartaches, along with the fierce winds of trials and tribulations. Winds and waves can knock you off course, slam you around, and leave you feeling frenzied, frazzled, fearful, and frustrated. Listen to the warnings. Act while there’s time make the necessary changes. Turn your life around so you won’t plow into any—or all—of the four dreadful icebergs: disappointment, defeat, discouragement, and devastation.

Use this guide to make the most of life’s challenges and opportunities this Lent. Read the reflections, do the activities, and say the prayers. They offer you a refreshing break from everything that makes you feel stressed, rushed, and overcommitted.

Let God minister to your heart in the gentlest of ways. Bask in the warmth of Jesus’ love, and welcome the healing he offers. Commit yourself to healthy change, and be willing to grow in different directions. In this way you’ll be better prepared to help yourself and others through deep waters.

TWENTY-THIRD PUBLICATIONS *A division of Bayard* • 977 Hartford Turnpike Unit A; Waterford, CT 06385
(860) 437-3012 or (800) 321-0411 • twentythirdpublications.com

ISBN: 978-1-62785-870-0 • Cover image: ©stock.adobe.com/julia
Printed in the U.S.A.

MIX
Paper | Supporting responsible forestry
FSC
www.fsc.org
FSC® C004755

JOEL 2:12–18 • 2 CORINTHIANS 5:20—6:2 • MATTHEW 6:1–6, 16–18

Catching Up

Go into your room, shut the door, and pray to your Father. MATTHEW 6:6

An explorer hired a crew to guide him through the Amazon rainforest. At first, the energetic crew hacked a path through the undergrowth. But on the third morning they just sat around. When asked why, a guide said, "They say they must wait until their souls catch up with their bodies."

What an apt metaphor for the way many of us live! Our bodies run so far ahead that our souls become disconnected. No wonder we feel frenzied, frazzled, fearful, and frustrated.

"When you pray," Jesus says, "go to your inner room." He wasn't referring to a location but to a place inside each of us where our bodies and souls are in sync. Ash Wednesday prepares us to enter that inner room by facing everything Jesus will bring to our attention during Lent. I have nuanced the lenten practices of fasting, almsgiving, and prayer to guide us once we're inside that inner room:

> *Fasting (Give It Up):* Few joys in life are greater than finding ways to overcome obstacles. By allowing Jesus' message to impact our lives, we give up these roadblocks. We reconnect body and soul by using healthy behavior to replace all that hinders our growth.
>
> *Almsgiving (Serve It Up):* We'll be asked to look inside ourselves for soul maintenance through simple activities, questions, and practices. Once our souls catch up with the rest of our selves, we'll become inspired, hopeful, self-confident, playful, and loving.
>
> *Prayer (Pray It Up):* Asking for help seems like a no-brainer, but we often hesitate. Surely we can release our sense of control long enough to turn our needs over to Jesus for soul nourishment, to feel Jesus' arms holding us as he whispers, "I'll take care of you."

This booklet will give you a break from what is difficult, stressful, and challenging in your life. Catching up is not easy or quick, but it is possible.

DEUTERONOMY 30:15–20 • LUKE 9:22–25

Me? No Way!

Follow me. LUKE 9:23

GIVE IT UP ▪ Michelangelo stood chiseling a huge, unsightly piece of granite. A passerby asked, "What are you doing?" He said, "I see an angel trapped in this rock, and I'm letting the angel out."

Have you wondered if you can ever be set free from the person you became? Although you may have made a thousand mistakes and feel like that old, rough rock, Jesus looks at you and says, "I see in you an angel, a child of God. Somebody I can use." As he helps remove the parts that aren't "angel," Jesus chips away at your life. It hurts, yes, but he must bring out the person trapped inside the rock.

When the world saw Jesus' disciples, they saw rough, smelly fishermen, despised tax collectors, and fanatical politicians. But Jesus saw people who could turn the world upside down with the gospel.

Jesus said, "You are Simon, but you shall be Peter." Think about what you shall be: a unique and special person. My value lies in the fact that I am me, and yours in the fact that you are you. Take comfort: there will always be people who accept you.

People often say to me, "Thanks for being you." My answer is, "I tried for years to be someone else. It didn't work."

SERVE IT UP ▪ Use Lent to seek out scared, sad, and shy people. Give them some inspiration—a quote, story, poem, or Bible passage—to ignite their spirits. Help set them free to believe in themselves. And for you: look in a mirror and say three positive things about yourself. Honor yourself with dignity and respect. Repeat daily.

PRAY IT UP ▪ *Jesus, as you continually fashion and form me into the person I ought to be, open my ears to hear your gentle voice whisper, "Follow me." Amen.*

ISAIAH 58:1–9A • MATTHEW 9:14–15

Enjoy It While You Can

The days will come when the bridegroom is taken away.... MATTHEW 9:15

GIVE IT UP ■ Nothing is more death-like than a life unlived. Deep down, most of us feel we should be able to live life wide open. We call this "passion." Too many of us are closed shut, passion-impaired. We can remember when our blood really pumped, when our heart skipped beats, and when there was some purpose toward which we reached with everything in us. What can make us eager to leap out of bed in the morning, filled with purpose, exhilarated about the prospect of another twenty-four hours on earth?

You'll find the secret on the bumper sticker slogan "*Carpe diem*," Latin words that mean "seize the day." We call this an imperative with a strong verb: seize it! The phrase implies immediacy, passion, gusto. The day is as fleeting as a deer in the woods. One moment of hesitation and it's gone forever. Jesus advises John's disciples: seize life! Don't let it go. Be ready to live it now, before it's too late.

Seize the day, in spite of all the critics and cynics who sit in the back row of life, whispering and rolling their eyes. We can't live our lives over again, but we can make progress from where we are to where God wants us to be. Seize the day! Life is meant to be a celebration. Wise is the person who finds a reason to make every day special.

SERVE IT UP ■ Write "*Carpe diem*" on index cards. Decorate the cards and pass them out to family and friends. Create a *carpe diem* post for social media. Encourage others to seize the day and to share the post with those in their lives.

PRAY IT UP ■ *Jesus, thank you for giving me this fresh, bright, gift-wrapped day. Amen.*

ISAIAH 58:9B–14 • LUKE 5:27–32

Messed Up? Fess Up!

Why do you eat and drink with tax collectors and sinners? LUKE 5:30

GIVE IT UP ▪ I've messed up in many areas of my life, and I will again. Sometimes I tried to be super mature in my own strength and fell flat on my face. Other times, I went to the other extreme, waiting for God to make me super mature without my making an effort. This also caused me to fall flat on my face.

When I do mess up, I fess up to a few close friends. Their empathy, love, and vulnerability encourage and strengthen me. So does their forgiveness when I admit my mistakes. Fess-up friends encourage us to say, "I messed up." It's a conversion to open our eyes, admit our blunders, and accept full responsibility.

Jesus was a fess-up friend; no wonder he had so many dinner invitations! At the table, he listened as if each speaker were the only one worth hearing. Jesus helped people see and accept their human imperfections, giving them room to admit their mistakes and strength to meet frustration and failure.

Fessing up enables us to be accountable, an essential component of our spiritual and emotional growth. We're always growing, gaining insights, and learning from our daily experiences. Our mess-ups can be some of life's greatest teachers—if we choose to learn from them rather than let them crush us. My mess-ups teach me dependence on God and enable me to learn about character, perseverance, and humility. What have your mess-ups taught you?

SERVE IT UP ▪ As you work to improve yourself during Lent, consider finding your own fess-up friend. Select this person from among people who know you the best—your spouse, pastor, or close friends.

PRAY IT UP ▪ *Jesus, help me to believe my mess-ups are never final but opportunities to fess up and do better next time. Amen.*

GENESIS 2:7–9; 3:1–7 • ROMANS 5:12–19 *or* 5:12, 17–19 • MATTHEW 4:1–11

Breakdown or Breakthrough?

Away with you, Satan! MATTHEW 4:10

GIVE IT UP ▪ I imagine that anyone fully alive has felt discouraged at one time or another. Phrases such as "It's not worth it," "I can't," "I give up," or "I've failed" are standard. Yet we need not censure ourselves for feeling discouragement. It's a very human attribute. It is important to remember that, no matter what circumstances brought us to this low point, they're not insurmountable.

When I was growing up, we lived through many circumstances that could have been devastating for the entire family. In spite of—or perhaps especially because of—those times, Mom and Dad never allowed us to lose our sense of humor, sense of self, or the assurance that we'd find a way to get through the hard times. Somehow, we always made it.

Every major discouragement we face in life is a fork in the road. We choose the track we will head down, toward breakdown or breakthrough. The truly healthy person discovers breakthroughs by having available the greatest number of alternatives for any discouragement. With choices, we feel less trapped and more in a position to decide what is best for us. Jesus and the devil faced off in the desert. For every attempt to break Jesus down, Jesus found a breakthrough and broke down the devil, rendering him powerless.

Discouragement at times seems inescapable, but to remain in this state is a waste of time, energy, and life. When we learn to put discouragement aside, we can get on with life. We are limited only by our willingness to discover these alternatives.

SERVE IT UP ▪ Call a friend to say how much you appreciate him or her for offering a solution you hadn't considered—one that didn't make sense at first.

PRAY IT UP ▪ *Jesus, thanks for the breakthroughs in my life when everything seemed upside down. Amen.*

LEVITICUS 19:1–2, 11–18 • MATTHEW 25:31–46

What Didn't I Do?

Lord, when was it that we saw you hungry or thirsty or a stranger or naked or sick or in prison, and did not take care of you? MATTHEW 25:44

GIVE IT UP ▪ Helping others is one of life's most rewarding experiences. We were brought up on barn raisings, bucket brigades, quilting bees, and bake sales. Telethons and fundraisers bring in countless dollars for Olympic teams, people with disabilities, and those who lack food.

Somehow we lose sight of the fact that need is ongoing. It's too easy to sit back and say, "I've done my bit."

We often associate giving with money, but can money equal the value of someone sitting with a dying person who would otherwise be alone? Or of someone who delivers a warm meal to an elderly, housebound individual? Or who volunteers to teach reading?

We become more visible or meaningful when we help someone else. What we do, after all, speaks clearly about who we are, what we believe, what we value, and how we feel about ourselves and our world.

The Chinese philosopher Lao Tzu wrote, "Kindness in words creates confidence, kindness in thinking creates profoundness, and kindness in giving creates love." And until love is manifested through some caring act, love is nothing more than a very good idea. We *can* do something. We become truly human the moment we reach out to help someone else.

SERVE IT UP ▪ Form a Coffee, Conversation, and Caring Group during Lent. Select a place to meet, make a pot of coffee, and begin with a prayer, allowing time for sharing needs. Perhaps next you can discuss a book, such as *The Five People You Meet in Heaven* by Mitch Albom. Then choose a need in your community or parish and decide how you or your group will help.

PRAY IT UP ▪ *Jesus, use me to do something meaningful for a needy brother or sister. Amen.*

ISAIAH 55:10–11 • MATTHEW 6:7–15

Bury the Hatchet, Handle and All

Forgive us our debts, as we forgive our debtors. MATTHEW 6:12

GIVE IT UP ▪ I've always found it difficult to bury the proverbial hatchet. It's tough enough to let it go even when the person says, "I'm sorry." But to forgive before you receive that apology—that seems impossible! When someone hurts us, we often lose perspective and want the scales tipped in our favor.

But we have choices. We can go our separate ways and never talk again; live with accusation, blame, and anger; bear grudges, nurse hate, or seek revenge; pretend everything is fine; bury our feelings; keep chewing on that hurt and never let it heal; or go face to face with the person, talk it through, and forgive.

Forgiveness only begins when we put pride aside and remember we live in this world with the wronged and wrongdoers. What's the hardest part of forgiving? Forgetting. When we don't deliberately forget about the hurt we've forgiven, we bury the hatchet but leave the handle sticking up. When someone reminds us of the past, that bitter taste creeps back into our mouths.

Let's stop dwelling on the past! Why allow hurt and harm to rent space inside our heads? Let the pain go by canceling the debt completely. It's the only way.

SERVE IT UP ▪ Write down the name of someone you've forgiven but whose deed you have a hard time forgetting. Include that person in your prayers. Then tear up or burn that paper to symbolize your desire to forget.

PRAY IT UP ▪ *Jesus, I know it's difficult to forgive others who have trespassed into my life and caused me damage, but it's the only way for me to have peace. Help me to love and forgive as you did. Amen.*

JONAH 3:1–10 • LUKE 11:29–32

Arms that Circle the Universe

This generation...asks for a sign. LUKE 11:29

GIVE IT UP ▪ In *One Hundred Years of Solitude*, Gabriel García Márquez tells of a village where people are afflicted with a kind of plague that causes them to forget the names of common everyday objects. One man, still unaffected, tries to limit the damage by labeling everything. "This is a table," "This is a cow; it must be milked every morning." At the town's entrance, he posts two large signs. One says, "The name of our village is Maconda." The larger sign says, "God exists."

We all forget much of what we've learned in life. That's OK. But if we forget to whom we belong, then our lives will be empty.

We often misperceive God and relate to a distorted image. For example, the "referee God" tallies points for good performance on a huge scoreboard in the sky. When we long for this God, we're terrified that we'll step out of line and suffer a penalty.

The one quality that describes God better than any other is love. To see God in the absence of love is a major obstacle in our efforts to develop an authentic relationship with God. God's love encourages us to get real by dumping everything out of our lives that warps, dilutes, or compromises the person we were meant to be, until only our genuine self remains.

Set aside time each day to bask in God's love—not just during Lent, but every day. Say, "I want to know you." Allow space for God to speak to you. But be forewarned: no one who falls in love with God ever stays the same.

SERVE IT UP ▪ In one sentence, summarize your faith journey and how it brought you to your present relationship with God. Share it with others.

PRAY IT UP ▪ *Jesus, I long to belong to you. Amen.*

ESTHER C:12, 14–16, 23–25 • MATTHEW 7:7–12

Hello, God? Are You There?

How much more will your Father in heaven give good things to those who ask him! MATTHEW 7:11

GIVE IT UP ■ Desperate people pray. They pray even if they're not sure to whom they're praying or if anyone is listening. It's fine to pray in a time of crisis, but desperate prayers alone don't sustain our spiritual life.

My greatest struggle with prayer was "Does God hear me?" Years ago, I was making a directed retreat at a Trappist monastery. During one of my conferences, a brother said, "All of heaven stops so the prayers of the saints can rise before God." Then it hit me. My prayers are heard. They matter so much that they interrupt heaven.

If you've been a desperate pray-er, Lent is a great opportunity to get in the habit of becoming a consistent pray-er by practicing the two Ps:

Period of time. Try five minutes a day. It's better to get a short time established than to begin with a longer period and give up later. Pray when you're at your best. Give God your best time.

Place for praying. Choose your "prayer-closet." A space used repeatedly will become sacred. My favorite place to meet God is in a prayer chair that's been bathed with tears and smiles over the decades.

God doesn't take off points for awkward pauses, poor grammatical construction, or unexpected emotional outbursts. Praying knits our hearts together with God's heart. Pray often. Then embrace the quiet and listen to God's answers.

SERVE IT UP ■ Want to get started praying? Take a prayer break instead of a coffee break.

PRAY IT UP ■ *Jesus, I know my prayers are important to you. I'm glad you're there. Amen.*

EZEKIEL 18:21–28 • MATTHEW 5:20–26

Tell Me: I Can Take It

Come to terms quickly with your accuser.... MATTHEW 5:25

GIVE IT UP ■ It's never easy to look someone directly in the eye and say, "I feel you have betrayed my trust." But unresolved problems in our relationships can result in unexplained distances, loss of mutual trust, fear, and avoidance. To be lovingly truthful with someone who has wronged us, we need to know when to speak and when to keep quiet, as well as courage to face the outcome of the confrontation. Sometimes our best efforts will be met with anger, denial, and avoidance. At those times, pray for guidance, try to be patient, and consider these four steps to mend the relationship:

Confidentially confront: Avoid sharing the issue with others who are not involved in the problem.

Come clean: Tell the truth, and don't hold back.

Continue caring: Approach the problem from a place of caring. Your words will be softer and your message more clearly heard.

Contact help: If you've been confidential, honest, and caring, and you still experience the same negative behavior, get in touch with a priest, therapist, or counselor so both sides are heard and weighed.

When Jesus talks about loving confrontation, his words apply to serious situations, not petty issues. If the wrongdoer won't change, forgive and forget.

SERVE IT UP ■ If you have an unresolved problem with someone, send them a message: "Our friendship is valuable to me. Can we resolve what stands between us?" Then use my four steps of making amends.

PRAY IT UP ■ *Jesus, help me to listen and to speak the truth when necessary. Amen.*

DEUTERONOMY 26:16–19 • MATTHEW 5:43–48

Do I Hafta?

Love your enemies and pray for those who persecute you. MATTHEW 5:44

GIVE IT UP ▪ In most classic works of fiction, the bad guys are pretty easy to discern. But what about the enemies in real life? Try this: love these people. This isn't easy, logical, or expected, yet Jesus teaches that we are to meet this challenge head-on. He said, "Turn hate upside down." If we have difficulty with this challenge, we're not alone. The people of Jesus' day didn't know what to do with Jesus' love-your-enemies commandment either. It's a radical teaching to "turn the other cheek" and to "love people who hate you."

In the real world, we reciprocate by giving insults back when people poke fun at us in front of others. We retaliate. These are natural reactions. But how can we love someone who hates us? Perhaps our "real world" solution isn't the best way to go. Why not try a different approach? H.A.T.E. is the answer.

Halt. Call for a cease-feuding. Stop the nastiness and name-calling.
Avoid. Stay away from situations that could be troublesome.
Truce. Look for common ground. Focus on areas of agreement.
Evaluate. What happened to drive a wedge in the relationship? Whatever the wrongdoing, address it. Seek a mutual solution.

It's a challenge to love your enemies—and nothing annoys them more!

SERVE IT UP ▪ The command to love your enemies is an absolute necessity for civilization's survival. Reflect on the challenge of loving people who rub you the wrong way. Come up with practical ways you can show love to an enemy. Talk to other people you know about what they do.

PRAY IT UP ▪ *Jesus, give me an extra helping of love for those I find difficult. Amen.*

GENESIS 12:1–4A • 2 TIMOTHY 1:8B–10 • MATTHEW 17:1–9

Get Real

Lord, it is good for us to be here. MATTHEW 17:4

GIVE IT UP ▪ Few people see the real us. We have special masks for work, home, and church. We're terrified of criticism, rejection, and intrusion. Our strongest urges are to control, to be loved unconditionally, and to have approval in every situation. When we go deep inside ourselves we can catch a glimpse of who we truly are, underneath the mask: God's child, spectacularly fashioned as a unique creation, splendidly crafted with authenticity and genuineness, stunningly designed to live life with joyfulness and wholeness.

Once you take off your mask and see the real you, you change completely. It's your moment of personal transfiguration, when your fears, feelings, desires, excitements, thoughts, and dreams—the sum total of which absolutely define you—are crisp and clear. It's contagious: once you remove your mask, others are likely to do the same. Your genuineness and authenticity build a bridge from one person to another.

To achieve wholeness, drop your guard, stop putting up a front, take off the costume and mask, and get real.

SERVE IT UP ▪ Get a paper bag, magazines, scissors, and a glue stick. Cut out words or pictures that describe the different masks you wear. Paste them all over the outside of the bag. Share your mask with someone you trust, and then ask yourself what you can do to discard the masks you sometimes wear.

PRAY IT UP ▪ *Jesus, you see the real me. You want me to stop pretending; help me to start peeling off my masks, place them at your feet, and become the real me. Amen.*

DANIEL 9:4B–10 • LUKE 6:36–38

Finding the Root Cause

Do not judge, and you will not be judged. LUKE 6:37

GIVE IT UP ▪ Lisa considers herself a perfectionist. "I set the bar high for others," she says, "but also for myself." Her judgments—often harsh—put a strain on many of her friendships.

A judgmental attitude stems from feelings of inferiority. It's easier to judge others than to experience and address our own pain. The result: we think we can make assumptions about others and analyze their behavior instead of our own. Incapable of taking control of our own lives, we try to manage other people's lives. We try to change the other person, unconsciously desiring to make ourselves feel more powerful.

To get past the judging, we need to give a voice to what we actually feel. This requires going inside ourselves and confronting ourselves until we find the root of the painful experience and begin to heal it.

Lisa realized that her judgmental attitude has hurt people. She looked inside and determined that the root cause of her pain was the criticism piled on her as she was growing up. Once she figured out the source of her pain, she taught herself not to judge others by her unrealistic standards.

A regular diet of judging someone will cause us to adopt an attitude toward that person that shuts down possibilities and smothers the insights of our heart. In two blunt and absolute words, Jesus commands us, "Stop judging."

SERVE IT UP ▪ It's soul-searching time. What do you think your judgmental behavior is covering up within yourself?

PRAY IT UP ▪ *Jesus, help me never to look down on anyone—unless I'm going to help them up. Amen.*

ISAIAH 1:10, 16–20 • MATTHEW 23:1–12

That's Not How I See You

All who exalt themselves will be humbled, and all who humble themselves will be exalted. MATTHEW 23:12

GIVE IT UP ▪ Nicholas, my widowed next-door neighbor, sat listening to his children. "You're seventy, Dad," they said. "Forget this crazy dream of finding a new life." He shocked them by going to polka parties and burning up the dance floor. Then he met a lovely lady and decided to remarry. He died three years later, while on a trip to a city he'd always dreamed of visiting. Nicholas fell peacefully into his wife's arms, smiling as he drew his last breath.

We can be chained to our perceptions of people, but they're seldom in sync with reality. Even the disciples had differing perceptions of Jesus. They told Jesus what other people perceived him to be: a prophet returning from the dead; Elijah; John the Baptist. Peter frees himself from people's perceptions and affirms the reality that Jesus is the Messiah.

Our perceptions can be like a set of chains that bind us to judgmental thinking. We have the key to be freed—all we need to do is change the way we look at people and form no opinions about others until we get to know them for ourselves. We may find that people like cousin Walter, who's always been perceived as a bore, or our neighbor, who is perceived as standoffish, are one day changed into kind, likable people—or perhaps it's we who changed in how we perceived them!

SERVE IT UP ▪ Think of a significant person in your life and the first time you met one another. What were your first impressions? How have they changed over time? What snapped your chains of perception to change your view of the person?

PRAY IT UP ▪ *Jesus, today I want to break the chains of how I see people. I want to see them as you see them, with eyes of love. Amen.*

JEREMIAH 18:18–20 • MATTHEW 20:17–28

Leaving the Nest

The mother of the sons of Zebedee came to him.... MATTHEW 20:20

GIVE IT UP ▪ Does your mother call you daily, telling you how to live your life? Are Mom and Dad still meddling in your business? It's time to cut the umbilical cord by leaving home psychologically.

Leaving home psychologically means different things to different people, but for everyone it means no longer viewing our parents as the dominating influence in our lives. Becoming a mature, healthy adult means you are ready to live your life on your terms and within your boundaries. We can only pass from childlike dependency to adult independence once we start thinking for ourselves, expressing what we are feeling, and standing firm in our decisions.

At first, it may be painful to claim your independence, so seek advice from a professional counselor or your parish priest. It's vital to establish boundaries with our parents, letting them know that although we love them very much, we will not allow them to tell us how to run our lives anymore. They may get upset when they are forced to respect our boundaries and honor our decisions, but we need to stand firm and refuse to let them intrude into our lives or play games with us.

Begin living your life today, absent of mother-father interference. You can survive without them—I promise.

SERVE IT UP ▪ Ask yourself, "Who is holding me back from leaving home?" Then write a declaration of independence to them (Mom, Dad, or another controlling person), claiming your unique individuality. Assert your freedom to become your own person, but don't send it. The declaration is for you alone.

PRAY IT UP ▪ *Jesus, I want to grow freely each day into the person you know I can be. Amen.*

JEREMIAH 17:5–10 • LUKE 16:19–31

Out of the Blue

He longed to satisfy his hunger with what fell from the rich man's table. LUKE 16:21

GIVE IT UP ▪ A server in an upscale Chicago bar, Colleen Gallagher, was struggling to make ends meet while she raised her two sons alone. One day, John Boc, the CEO of an investment company, was a patron at her establishment. While visiting with business associates, Boc also spoke with Gallagher, who was serving their table. He quickly realized that she was, in his words, "feeling blue."

When it came time to pay, Boc told Gallagher to add a $1,000 tip to the tab. Stunned and unsure, she prepared the credit card slip as he'd requested, and Boc signed it—but that's only the beginning. As tears began pouring down Colleen's face, Boc pulled a handful of credit cards from his pocket, fanned them like playing cards, and said, "Pick a card." When she took his Platinum Visa, he said, "Take that card and give yourself $10,000. Life's too short to be feeling blue."

Not many of us can gift someone $11,000, but we can make a difference in other people's lives. Smiles, a pat on the back, helping with a chore, or listening when someone needs you are good kindness starters. Watch what happens: kindness becomes contagious.

SERVE IT UP ▪ Play the "Who Dunnit?" game. Each family member thinks of a time when someone in the family was kind. The first person to speak explains what kindness was shown, and the others must guess "Who dunnit?" The person who guesses correctly is the next one to relate a kindness. If your family is small, you can share acts of kindness by grandparents and friends.

PRAY IT UP ▪ *Jesus, may I always sow kindness so many people can reap its benefits. Amen.*

GENESIS 37:3–4, 12–13A, 17B–28A • MATTHEW 21:33–43, 45–46

Taming the Green-Eyed Monster

This is the heir; let us kill him and get his inheritance. MATTHEW 21:38

GIVE IT UP ▪ We all compare ourselves with our friends occasionally, but if you can't think about someone's expensive car, good-looking partner, or exotic vacations without feeling bitter, it's time to tackle that green-eyed monster. Envy does not respect social position, intellectual capacity, economic level, or age. Envy can be a positive or negative force in our lives, depending upon how we act on what we feel. Donna's envy of Cathy's weight loss inspired Donna to ditch her candy habit and hit the gym more frequently.

People who are free from envy savor what they have. Their cravings for power, fame, and fortune are almost nonexistent. Ask them what they need, and they'll respond, "Nothing," or "Not much." It's different with the envious. The green-eyed monster starts gnawing at their hearts and souls, redirecting their attention from their blessings and onto what they see in someone else's life.

Envious people set their hearts on other people's possessions, popularity, and lifestyles. What can we do to keep envy away? We move our focus from someone else's life to our own lives. This changes our focus from what we've lost to what we've gained—from where we've failed to where we can succeed. This leaves no room for envy.

SERVE IT UP ▪ Create a Bucket of Blessings. (Use a small jar or container for a bucket.) Each day, on a piece of paper or index card, write out at least one good thing in your life or blessing you have received, and drop it into the bucket. Encourage your friends and family to make their own Bucket of Blessings.

PRAY IT UP ▪ *Jesus, direct my heart away from someone else's life and onto my own so I can recognize and appreciate the blessings you lovingly splash all over me. Amen.*

MICAH 7:14–15, 18–20 • LUKE 15:1–3, 11–32

Counting to Ten

Then he became angry and refused to go in. **LUKE 15:28**

GIVE IT UP ▪ Excitement energizes the homecoming of the prodigal son. Everyone is happy except the older brother, who's angry about the whole thing.

While anger is a normal emotion, we need to tame it so we're not always ready to blow up. Here are three ways we can respond when something triggers our anger:

Cool the flames. When you approach the boiling point, use a simple relaxation tool, such as deep breathing, to help calm angry feelings. Picture your breath coming up from your diaphragm while you slowly repeat a word or phrase like "relax" or "take it easy."

Change our thoughts. When we're angry, we tend to think critical thoughts about ourselves or others. Try replacing these thoughts with more positive, rational ones. Create fresh thoughts and solutions. Put control back in your life.

Communicate directly after we've calmed down. Once you're calm, speak clearly to the person(s) involved about whatever is frustrating you. Talk about your feelings and perceptions, rather than blaming others or assuming you know what's going on with them. Listen to what the other person says. Take time before responding.

In order to live a joyful, balanced life, we must learn to deal with anger.

SERVE IT UP ▪ Make "anger tamers," little signs with phrases such as "Count to ten," "Take it easy," or "Jesus, help me!" Place them in visible locations in your home. Look at them whenever you feel your anger rising.

PRAY IT UP ▪ *Jesus, enlighten me so I don't allow anger to control me as I prepare to confront a situation. Amen.*

EXODUS 17:3–7 • ROMANS 5:1–2, 5–8 • JOHN 4:5–42 *or* 4:5–15, 19B–26, 39A, 40–42

The Eyes Have It

Sir, I see that you are a prophet. JOHN 4:19

GIVE IT UP ■ Have you ever wished you could just disappear? I'm sure the woman at the well felt this way when Jesus walked into her life. Her life is in shambles: she has either dumped or been dumped by five husbands and is working on her sixth. Yet Jesus' eyes don't criticize or condemn. His gaze invites her to say words that release her hurt and loneliness. Jesus invites her to break down her façade so his words can unleash their unlimited power to heal and restore.

Since most of us have learned to adopt an "I-can-do-it-myself" attitude, we often find it difficult to tell others we need their help. When we hurt inside, we too often put on a plastic smile, one that says we're at peace when we're retching inside. Caring people engage in eyeball-to-eyeball contact. They get inside our worlds and see beyond our masks. They break down the walls of the hiding places we've built brick by brick. They connect soul to soul, their gazes shouting, "Let me come in to where you are." What follows bridges the space that often expands between people but is easily joined with words like "I understand," "Forget about it," "It's going to get better," and "I'm sticking with you."

It's time to lift our heads and see who's waiting to look into our eyes. Today can be a new beginning, if we only open our hearts to someone.

SERVE IT UP ■ Make the first day of each month your special day—pamper yourself. Throw off your problems. Claim peace. You deserve these bonus days. Give them to yourself.

PRAY IT UP ■ *Jesus, with your help I can be your eyes, spotting those who are hurting and broken. Amen.*

2 KINGS 5:1–15AB • LUKE 4:24–30

Only I Can Fill My Shoes

They got up and drove him out of the town.... **LUKE 4:29**

GIVE IT UP ▪ Jesus is back in his old neighborhood: the local hero returning home. But people aren't lining the streets. Some wear granite faces. Others roll their eyes, whispering among themselves comments full of biting sarcasm. Jesus didn't allow the cold reception or arrogance to affect him. He said what needed to be said and moved on.

Jesus teaches a valuable lesson we need to remember when people mock, shun, exclude, or just plain ignore us: avoid the "Takeover Twins," whose names are "Makin'" and "Fakin'." These negative forces cause us to make fun of others and put on a fake face to please people. The twins make us afraid that someone will be upset with us for expressing our needs. Hang out with the twins long enough, and they'll shape us into judgmental, condescending, negative, and arrogant people—all in the name of seeking approval.

It's impossible to be who you want to be and do what you want to do when you hang out with Makin' and Fakin'. We worry more about what others believe about us than what we know to be true. We become emotionally dishonest with our feelings. Make a deal with yourself during this season of Lent: decide to stop spending time with the Takeover Twins, and learn to believe you don't have to keep working to buy people's love.

SERVE IT UP ▪ You only have one life to live—yours. Here are two ways to live in a healthy and holy way. Say "no" when you need to, when you are overwhelmed by the demands of others and have no time for yourself. Say "yes" to life, to discovering the beauty that God holds out to us in the ordinary events and times of our lives.

PRAY IT UP ▪ *Jesus, stand beside me as I stand tall, courageously living my own life. Amen.*

DANIEL 3:25, 34–43 • MATTHEW 18:21–35

Forgive? Not a Chance!

How often should I forgive? MATTHEW 18:21

GIVE IT UP ■ Sometimes the end of a relationship is so ugly that the only antidote seems to be revenge. But Lent is a time to wipe the slate clean. Each experience with a person is nothing more than a thought you carry around. You must release all the pain and bitterness by wholeheartedly forgiving everyone who's ever done you any wrong.

Don't even try to sweep your feelings under the rug and act as if they don't exist, or deny the fact that something bad happened. Eventually, all the anger and resentment you keep pushing down will rise to the surface and cause you problems, hurting you and those you love.

Do you refuse to deal with the issues God keeps bringing up? Too much anger and hatred? Too many painful memories? To heal, you need to get everything out in the open. It's been buried long enough. Give yourself the go-ahead to dig it all out.

Be the first to forgive. When you do, you'll no longer feel restless, cold, and irritable. You'll be able to make a fresh start in your life and will be happier as a direct result.

SERVE IT UP ■ Listen to God tugging at your heartstrings. Make a list of people for whom you feel anger or resentment. Write each person a letter. Explain how hurt you were, but take responsibility for each of your actions that contributed to the problem. Forgive that person, in writing. Mail the letters or throw them away—the act of forgiveness is in the writing.

PRAY IT UP ■ *Jesus, I was wronged. I want to forgive, but I can't do this on my own. With your help, I can choose to forgive everybody who's ever hurt me. Amen.*

DEUTERONOMY 4:1, 5–9 • MATTHEW 5:17–19

Sailing to a Decision

Whoever does these commandments and teaches them will be called great in the kingdom of heaven. MATTHEW 5:19

GIVE IT UP ▪ How would Jesus navigate a sea of options and arrive at wise decisions for living a meaningful life? With the Ten Commandments. If we use them as our compass, we'll be able to steer toward the shore and be securely anchored. This overview can help us understand the commandments:

Reverencing God and all God's images by never cursing or condemning, slandering or slamming, rumoring or gossiping.
Respecting the people who have crossed our lives, touching us with love as they journey with us through difficulty and disappointment.
Remembering that the gift of life is precious and living it with purpose and joy, not with regret and doubts.
Refusing to allow prestige, power, position, and possessions to rob us of goodness, humility, service, and kindness.
Resisting the temptation to ruin relationships by neglect, untruthfulness, and unfaithfulness.
Realizing it takes years to build trust and only seconds to destroy it.
Relinquishing all cravings for other people's blessings.

Each day brings new opportunities. Choose wisely, and our lives will reach safe harbor. Choose foolishly, and we'll go down with the ship.

SERVE IT UP ▪ Since decisions are too important to leave to chance, what compass do you use to make sure you're headed in the right direction?

PRAY IT UP ▪ *Jesus, with you as my copilot, I will never be lost. Thank you. Amen.*

JEREMIAH 7:23–28 • LUKE 11:14–23

De-Ignite Dissension

Every kingdom divided against itself becomes a desert.... LUKE 11:17

GIVE IT UP ▪ There will always be differences within our relationships. Some we'll solve; some we'll manage. Others may be insurmountable. While big problems usually cause a relationship to collapse, a series of small things over a long period can ignite dissension. The results? Division. Damage to our relationships. Little inconsiderate behaviors, thoughtless comments, small cruel acts, words left unspoken, or well-intended acts that are constantly put off for later: all contribute to the end of our relationships.

Think about whether these types of comments are heard in your house: "He never picks up after himself"; "As soon as I get in the door, she starts with a litany of disasters"; "He eats dinner and then plops down in front of the TV and falls asleep. It's like living alone"; "She's constantly changing her mind."

Are any of these complaints earth-shattering? No. Relationships don't come apart overnight—they slowly crumble because we allow minor complaints to fester and don't want to correct our problems. We need the courage make our relationships stronger.

SERVE IT UP ▪ Are you a relationship breaker: complaining, demanding, arrogant, insensitive, fault-finding, belittling, controlling, or ridiculing? Or do you contribute to relationship build-up? Have you learned the importance of talking and listening, respecting needs, giving second chances, telling the truth, sharing your vulnerability, and working to end self-defeating behaviors? Use these days of reflection to keep relationships free from dissension and division.

PRAY IT UP ▪ *Jesus, I'm at my best when my relationships are working. Keep nudging me to grow together with those I love, not apart from them. Amen.*

HOSEA 14:2–10 • MARK 12:28–34

I'm Still Standing

Blasphemy against the Spirit will not be forgiven. MATTHEW 12:31

GIVE IT UP How do we weather life's storms? Here's one man's story. He failed in business twice, ran for state legislature and for Congress twice. And failed. He was defeated twice in Senate races. He worked hard to become vice president of the United States: no success. The young woman he loved died. He had a nervous breakdown. But he had the self-knowledge and strength to overcome adversity, carry on, and become president. His name: Abraham Lincoln.

Defeat and discouragement can dampen our spirits and leave us ready to give up. Sometimes we're blindsided by something life-shattering. We can't minimize the experience of a catastrophe. But we can recognize that the way we face the unexpected will make a significant difference in how we weather the storm.

Write down the name of the hurt that is bringing on despair. Add specific examples of how this hurt has occupied your mind. Include what you're feeling. Wrestle with your hurt. Get to know it. Look for its hidden secrets: promised blessings yet to come. Then confront your hurt. Ask, "What am I learning from it?" Then make the changes needed to grow in new directions.

Wipe out the hurt completely by ditching all the negative feelings before they get the best of you. Determine today that you will suffer only long enough to acknowledge the pain of your situation, but not so long that you get comfortable in your hurt. We can't help it when it hurts, but we can help it if the hurt lasts.

SERVE IT UP Take your hurt off life support. Declare it dead. Send a note to a hurting friend, offering your availability to listen.

PRAY IT UP *Jesus, trying times are times for me to try to have more faith. I'm trying! You're helping. Amen.*

HOSEA 6:1–6 • LUKE 18:9–14

Press On

God, be merciful to me, a sinner! LUKE 18:13

GIVE IT UP ▪ I recall teaching a bright high school senior whose mother was a perfectionist. After the student got an A in religion, I asked if she was pleased with the mark. "Yes," she said softly, "but my mother won't be. She'll want to know why it isn't an A+."

God didn't put us here to do everything "just right" or to be one another's monitors and critics, like the Pharisee, who felt he needed no improvement and looked down his nose at the tax collector. Trying to be perfect is a great tragedy. Once we admit and own our helplessness and powerlessness by accepting our limitations, growth in a genuine healthy relationship with Jesus is possible. Helen Keller, the great lady who lived in deafness and blindness, said, "I thank God for my limitations, for through them I have found myself, my work, and my God."

The high school students in my parish formed a club called "SIGN" (Service in God's Name). Once a month, they'd visit people with special needs, and I went along with them on these trips. The individuals with special needs taught me new meanings for "will" and "determination." Those who were blind learned to see with their fingers and their imaginations, using what they had to compensate for what they lacked.

All of us have this power: naturally or by acquiring it. Admitting our limits means we accept our imperfections and want to move ahead.

SERVE IT UP ▪ It doesn't matter what your limitations are; the only way to improve is to take action. Try. Even though your effort may seem insignificant. Reflecting on a relationship with Jesus helps you see possibilities beyond your limitations.

PRAY IT UP ▪ *Jesus, I am ready and eager to look my limitations in the face and try. Amen.*

1 SAMUEL 16:1B, 6–7, 10–13A • EPHESIANS 5:8–14 • JOHN 9:1–41 *or* 9:1, 6–9, 13–17, 34–38

Words Just Get in the Way

I went and washed and received my sight. JOHN 9:11

GIVE IT UP ■ Sam's wife was in intensive care, so he called me and said, "I need you." When I arrived, I spotted Sam sitting in the lounge, looking small and alone. When he saw me, his tears overflowed. What are the right words in a situation like that? What words of wisdom or Scripture should you recite? I learned an important lesson that night. Sometimes God's wisdom doesn't use words! I hugged him, held his hand, and wept with him. He needed compassion, not words.

When words fail us in our efforts to understand and be understood, reaching out with a hug or gentle touch is often our most direct and eloquent form of communication. There is something very explicit about one person surrounding another in a warm embrace. It's difficult to misinterpret a loving touch.

Blind from birth, the man didn't come looking for a sermon—he came looking for sight. And he received it. The gentle touch of Jesus opened his eyes, giving him his first glimpse of people and animals, sunrises and sunsets, the moon and the stars, trees and leaves, mountains and rivers. Awesome!

Touch is the most intimate of our senses. In reaching out to others, the message is clear: "I'm here, I'm close, and I care." It's sad that many of us wait a lifetime to discover the miraculous power of touch.

SERVE IT UP ■ Who do you run to when the bottom drops out in your life? Create your "safe haven" list. Write down the names of the people you can cry with as they hold you and hug you: not preaching to you, but listening, understanding, and saying, "I've been there, too."

PRAY IT UP ■ *Jesus, nothing can replace the security of intimate friends helping me to see past my heartaches. I am so grateful for them. Amen.*

ISAIAH 65:17–21 • JOHN 4:43–54

Where Do Broken Hearts Go?

Sir, come down before my little boy dies. JOHN 4:49

GIVE IT UP ▪ I spotted the tent and peeked inside. It was set up for a church revival. Someone said, "Come back tonight and listen to Brother Edward." That evening, God spoke to me through Brother Edward. My mother's recent death had me struggling, and his words guided me toward healing.

Let me share the five steps we experience in our efforts to give our problems completely to God—from Brother Edward, to me, and to you.

> *Churn.* When life rises up to knock us flat, a knife to the heart appropriately expresses what we're feeling inside.
>
> *Burn.* As shock wears away, anger steps forward.
>
> *Yearn.* We look to the past when everything was going well.
>
> *Learn.* Pain and grief have a way of making our hearts more compassionate and loving.
>
> *Turn.* Drop your pain into God's lap. Three words changed me: "Help me, God." I turned it over to God and felt extreme comfort.

I go through many of these stages repeatedly. I reach the fifth stage, and believe I've given it to God, and the next day a memory of Mom pushes me back to churning and burning. But it happens less frequently. One day my pain will ease, as long as I continue to give it over to God.

SERVE IT UP ▪ Create time to write down your experiences in going through the five steps of emotional pain. Write for as long as you can. Then give everything to God.

PRAY IT UP ▪ *Jesus, help me to believe that when those I love die, they're hidden in your heart so they may be closer to mine. Amen.*

EZEKIEL 47:1–9, 12 • JOHN 5:1–16

Worn-out Shoes

I have no one to put me into the pool.... JOHN 5:7

GIVE IT UP ▪ Some of us might remember "Grandfather's Corner," the Brothers Grimm story of an old man who lived with his son and family. Almost deaf and blind, the man had difficulty eating without spilling his food. Finally, the son and daughter-in-law gave him an unbreakable wooden bowl and made him eat in a corner behind the stove. One day, while the old man's grandson was working with some pieces of wood, his father asked what he was doing. "I'm making a trough for you and mother to eat out of when I'm grown up," he said. Immediately, his grandfather rejoined the family at the table. No one ever said another word about it.

When life knocks us off our feet, we say, "Put yourself in my shoes." Empathy allows us to step outside ourselves and try to understand another person from within. Since all of us have known rejection and failure, we're better able to understand the disappointment and despair of others. Through empathy, not only do we feel with others, but we're also less apt to judge them.

For thirty-eight years, our blind brother in today's gospel was treated like he was part of the landscape. People passed him by; some pushed him out of their way. Jesus connects with our brother's need by immediately asking him a simple question: "Do you want to be well?" Jesus helps us realize that we, too, may be in need of his help one day. Of all the human qualities that make us feel connected to each other, it's the ability to empathize that most draws us together.

SERVE IT UP ▪ Practice empathy's slogan: "Put yourself in my shoes." Before speaking or doing something, ask yourself, "How would I feel if this were said or done to me?"

PRAY IT UP ▪ *Jesus, let me never judge another person until I have worn out their shoes by walking in them for miles. Amen.*

ISAIAH 49:8–15 • JOHN 5:17–30

A One-way Ticket to Paradise

Anyone who hears my word and believes...has eternal life. **JOHN 5:24**

GIVE IT UP ▪ Each year I ask my high school seniors what they would do if they only had three days to live. Most want to do something that would make their lives complete. Then I ask, "Why do we wait? Why not now?"

The awareness of death is a healthy reminder to:

Dump the freight. Why worry about all the stuff we've accumulated over the years? Use the china you've been keeping for the grandchildren: they don't want it.

Stop the wait. I've never read the obituary of a person who died from an overdose of hugs and kisses. Death teaches us we don't have forever to say and show "I love you." Ask yourself: "Who in my life is love starved?" Visit, call, text, hug, or kiss them.

Don't be late. The tragedy in life is to reach the end without ever having really lived at all. How sad to see people who—fearing that the end is near—try to cram all the living and loving they can into the short time left. Don't be one of them.

When Jesus calls us home, we're not going to need eyeglasses, hearing aids, or credit cards. And we won't bring any emotional baggage. We'll be content, knowing we didn't put off all the things we ever wanted to do.

SERVE IT UP ▪ Downsize. Simplify your closets, cellar, attic, and garage. Ask yourself, "Do I need all this stuff?" Have a yard sale and give the money to a soup kitchen or food pantry.

PRAY IT UP ▪ *Jesus, why should I allow earthly cares to bring me down? Remind me that when I come home, they'll be a distant memory. Amen.*

March 19 ✝ Thursday of the Fourth Week
SAINT JOSEPH

2 SAMUEL 7:4–5A, 12–14A, 16 • ROMANS 4:13, 16–18, 22 • MATTHEW 1:16, 18–21, 24A *or* LUKE 2:41–51A

Detour Ahead

Joseph, son of David, do not be afraid to take Mary as your wife. MATTHEW 1:20

GIVE IT UP ▪ Everything was going fine for Mary and Joseph: they were in love. They looked forward to getting married and raising a family. Surprise! God had a different plan. Their assent to becoming part of God's incredible plan taught them a lesson from which we can all benefit: life is uncertain.

Life's surprises will always surprise us. The only way we can deal with these uncertainties is to have *faith* and *faces* that prop us up:

> *Faith*. When we're hit with the unexpected, we must first believe God is big enough to take care of us. We must ask God to give us what we need to overcome anxiety, fear, worry, and all lingering concerns. God won't disappoint us.
>
> *Faces*. Then we must look for the faces of those who can prop us up when we're unable to stand alone. At different times, we're each called to be "propper-uppers," building up others with positive words and uplifting actions.

It's easy to collapse when we're hit with the unexpected. Yet if we do, we might find ourselves—near the end of our lives—thinking: *If I'd had more faith in God, what might I have done? If I'd reached out further, what might I have become?*

SERVE IT UP ▪ Give up an activity you enjoy. Use the time to talk with a friend or neighbor who could use some propping up.

PRAY IT UP ▪ *Jesus, you have given me two hands—one for receiving help and the other for giving help. Remind me to use both. Amen.*

WISDOM 2:1A, 12–22 • JOHN 7:1–2, 10, 25–30

Leaping Off Roofs

You know me, and you know where I am from. JOHN 7:28

GIVE IT UP ▪ One night, a young boy was forced to climb out on the roof when his house caught fire. From the ground, his father called, "Jump! I'll catch you!" The boy protested, "Daddy, I can't see you." The father shouted back, "But I can see you!"

Trust is vital for a wholesome relationship. When we say, "I don't trust you," we keep each other at a distance. We build walls, saying, "That's far enough: don't come any closer." Jesus came into a world of suspicious, reluctant, and cynical people. No trust. Every word was commented on; every action was criticized.

What a difference when we say, "I trust you." Trust doesn't happen all at once. The deeper we grow, the more we reveal about ourselves. It's a comfort to have one person we can run to when it falls apart—we trust that their love will accept us and give us the room to cry, yell, and scream. They let us get it all out and stick by us as we put our lives back together and go on living.

We can have the same relationship with Jesus. It begins with two simple words: "I surrender." The relationship with him will deepen when we say, "Jesus, I need you." Speak from your heart: "Jesus, I need you for direction and guidance. Help me make the right decision." "Jesus, I need you for courage and strength." "Jesus, I need you for spunk and grit: help me to keep on going." Jesus will give us all we need.

SERVE IT UP ▪ Surrender. Invite Jesus inside your life. Once he's inside, there's no need to be afraid. Jesus will say, "I know everything about you. It doesn't matter. I love you." Tell Jesus what's going on in your life. Leave nothing out.

PRAY IT UP ▪ *Jesus, help me hold no problem back—nothing large, nothing small. When you say, "Surrender," I know you want it all. Amen.*

JEREMIAH 11:18–20 • JOHN 7:40–53

I'll Never Budge!

There was a division in the crowd because of him. JOHN 7:43

GIVE IT UP ▪ When Bernice came to see me, she was upset. "From September through January, he plops himself in front of the TV and watches one football game after another. When I complain, he tells me to sit down and watch: I might develop an interest in football. He even offered to take me to an Eagles' game on bobble-head day!" I suggested that Bernice compromise. "No way!" she replied. I'm positive that with serious, honest dialogue, just a little movement toward each other, there would be a solution—or at least a little better understanding.

Many of us refuge to budge. Right or wrong, we dig in our heels and take our stand. We put on stone faces and use phrases such as "Over my dead body" or "Not until hell freezes over."

Jesus runs into a brick wall when he encounters a crowd of "no-way-am-I-going-to-see-it-differently" attitudes over the origins of the Messiah, so we're not alone. A good compromise is one of the simplest ways to affirm and grow in the love and mutual respect that is vital to lasting relationships. Perhaps during Lent, it would be good to consider the "nevers"—all the indisputable "no-way-am-I-going-to-change" attitudes we develop and permanently add to our personalities.

SERVE IT UP ▪ Many people don't rise to compromise because they don't want to bend. If you tend to be unyielding, write down this phrase and keep it where you can see it every day: "Not why I can't bend, but how I can bend." To bring about healthy, livable resolution, look for ways to reach some middle ground.

PRAY IT UP ▪ *Jesus, move me to openness and away from stubbornness. Amen.*

EZEKIEL 37:12–14 • ROMANS 8:8–11 • JOHN 11:1–45 *or* 11:3–7, 17, 20–27, 33B–45

No Unheard Cries

Many came to Martha and Mary to console them.... JOHN 11:19

GIVE IT UP ▪ January 10, 2003—12:47 a.m. One moment I was anticipating my mom's recovery from open-heart surgery, and the next I learned she was in the presence of God. Afterward, driving with my sister to her house, I kept hearing the doctor's voice: "Father, I did all I could. You mom's heart was too weak. I'm sorry." Crawling into bed, I thought, *This must be a bad dream*. But it wasn't. Our mom was dead.

The next day, my sister received a package marked "Damaged in transit but deliverable." The string was hanging, the label missing, and books stuck out of one corner. Generally, I wouldn't have given the "Damaged" label a second thought, but the day it arrived my heart was broken. That package connected to my hurt. Jesus knew I needed something to remind me that there are things in life I can't do anything about. Jesus says, "I know you've been damaged in transit, but don't stop there. Read the rest: still deliverable."

We journey at our own paces, from "damaged" to "deliverable." Our journeys will be easier if we remain open to the things that connect to our hurt. For me, it was a package label; a movie starring Angelina Jolie, *Life or Something Like It*, gently reminding that time and people are precious; a sermon by Brother Edward, urging me to turn my hurt over to God; a song by Celine Dion, "My Heart Will Go On." I refuse to let life's tragedies define me and destroy me. By which reminders will *your* journey be defined?

SERVE IT UP ▪ When troubles damage you in transit, make a list of everything you can't do anything about and acknowledge that Jesus can. Post it on your bathroom mirror. Add items as necessary.

PRAY IT UP ▪ *Jesus, I believe you hear my cries when I am damaged and hurt. Thank you. Amen.*

DANIEL 13:1–9, 15–17, 19–30, 33–62 *or* 13:41C–62 • JOHN 8:1–11

A Way Out

Jesus bent down and wrote with his finger on the ground. JOHN 8:6

GIVE IT UP ▪ I love the *Shrek* movies for their clean humor and moral messages. Shrek, a no-nonsense ogre, believes he should be alone because he's ugly. Many agree without ever getting to know him. The movies carry an important message: take time to get to know people before making judgments about them.

Jesus comes face to face with an angry mob of Pharisees who bring him a woman they want to stone to death. They dragged this frightened woman into a corner, piled up charges and false judgments against her, and eagerly waited for Jesus to say, "Kill her." But when Jesus bent down to write in the sand, he turned everything upside down, forcing the Pharisees to leave.

What did Jesus write? I think he was scribbling and doodling, thinking, *They just don't get it. It's about second chances. Changing and growing.* It's about conversion and not condemning. It's about the present and not the past. It's about forgiving, not finger pointing. It's about choosing to be a life-lifter, not a life-sinker.

Life-sinkers don't care about us but prefer to humiliate us by remembering and recycling our mistakes and failures, preventing us from moving on with our lives. Life-lifters show how much they care. They liberate us from people's negative comments and wrongful judgments, thus setting us free to be ourselves.

Every time we give someone a lift, we get a lift. Lift and be lifted: try it.

SERVE IT UP ▪ During the week, write thank-you notes to those life-lifters who have set you free from the crowd of life-sinkers. Write on!

PRAY IT UP ▪ *Jesus, I could easily switch places with the frightened woman you freed. Thank you for seeing who I really am. Amen.*

NUMBERS 21:4–9 • JOHN 8:21–30

How Delicious!

When you have lifted up the Son of Man, then you will realize that I am he. JOHN 8:28

GIVE IT UP ▪ As a monk is chased by three bears, he reaches the edge of a cliff. He jumps, and as he falls, he grabs hold of a clump of wood extending from the cliff. He looks down and sees three starving lions. In front of him, he sees three gophers. They're stretching out from their cliffside burrow, busily chewing away on the branch from which he's hanging. Looking just beyond them, he spots a juicy red strawberry. He plucks it, pops it in his mouth, and murmurs, "How delicious!"

How often we find ourselves replaying the events of the day at the dinner table, mulling over "what ifs" and "should have saids" as we absentmindedly eat. In fact, most of us are so intent on looking forward or backward that we go through much of life as if in a dream. Why not take a cue from our cheerful monk? With hungry bears above, starving lions below, and nibbling gophers facing him, he still manages to live in the moment, enjoying everything life gives him.

Life would be unbearable if we didn't have the opportunity of a fresh start each day. God gives us 365 days every year. God made every day to be a new day, a moment never seen before, a chance to live and say, "How delicious!"

SERVE IT UP ▪ Each of us owns a bank. Its name is TIME. Every morning, it credits you with 86,400 seconds. Every night, it writes off as lost the number of seconds you failed to invest to good purpose. You must live in the present on today's deposits. Invest in it to get from it the utmost in health, happiness, and success. The clock's running! Make the most of today.

PRAY IT UP ▪ *Jesus, you call yourself I Am, not I Was or I'm Gonna Be. Help me to live in the precious present—always. Amen.*

March 25 ✝ Wednesday of the Fifth Week

THE ANNUNCIATION OF THE LORD

ISAIAH 7:10–14; 8:10 • HEBREWS 10:4–10 • LUKE 1:26–38

Break Free

For nothing will be impossible for God. LUKE 1:37

GIVE IT UP ▪ Have you ever felt chained to a bad habit or destructive behavior? Listen to the wonderful words in Luke's gospel: "For nothing will be impossible for God." Although we might feel bound in chains, we have the ability to break free. And the feeling of freedom can be incredible. Before we can break free, however, we must understand a simple truth: nothing is impossible to get past.

Many people willingly place chains around themselves, all because of negative thinking. We cling to our past mistakes and struggles. We allow ourselves to be busy with critical and condemning input—not just from the naysayers in our lives, but also from our own minds. Don't listen to those who tell us our problems are too much for us to handle. We are the only ones who can decide what we're capable of. We must find out where the problems are leading us. Sometimes it's toward opportunities and possibilities we've overlooked.

Let's break free of chains that restrain us from realizing our highest potential. Let's believe in what we can do and what we can become. With every step we take, we leave the broken chains of yesterday further behind. Chains or change? It's a choice. If the desire to break our chains is strong enough, we can do it. We're bound only by our attitudes. And the attitude is "I can"; the words are "I will." Our greatest need is to believe that anything is possible.

SERVE IT UP ▪ What chains in your life need to be broken today? Make a list of everything that holds you back from realizing your potential and determine how you can break each link of each chain.

PRAY IT UP ▪ *Jesus, through the power of your love, I'm changing into a free person. Thanks! Amen.*

GENESIS 17:3–9 • JOHN 8:51–59

Endless Hope

Whoever keeps my word will never see death. JOHN 8:51

GIVE IT UP ▪ One of the saddest epitaphs I ever read appears on the headstone of Mel Blanc, the creative voice of so many famous cartoon characters, including Porky Pig and Elmer Fudd: "Th-th-th-that's all folks!" I don't know what Mel Blanc personally believed about life after death, but this life *isn't* all, folks; there is so much more. We don't face a hopeless end. We have an endless hope.

What will it be like to be in God's presence? Indescribable. Will we recognize our parents, spouses, children, and friends? Yes, and you will be yourself. What we do here, now, determines what comes after. Most people long to love and be loved. To feel worthwhile. We all want our lives to matter. They will—but only when we help make the lives of others complete.

Let's be pipelines for Jesus' love by using our God-given potential to pour into empty lives simple gestures that add meaning: give a smile to someone who is down; encourage the dreamer who has given up; speak a healing word to a brokenhearted person; light a candle of hope in the midst of another's dark night. There's no limit to the lives we can touch.

With Lent quickly coming to an end, hopefully we have seized the many opportunities to make a difference in the lives of others. Then, when the day comes that we stand before the Carpenter from Nazareth and tell him how we left the place we lived better off, he will whisper in our ear, "Well done."

SERVE IT UP ▪ Make a list of all the gestures you used during Lent that had a positive impact on people's lives. Continue filling the empty spaces in people's lives long after Lent is over.

PRAY IT UP ▪ *Jesus, nudge me to remember that the more I reach out to others, the more I enrich my own life. Amen.*

JEREMIAH 20:10–13 • JOHN 10:31–42

Put Cotton in Your Ears

They took up rocks to stone him. JOHN 10:31

GIVE IT UP ▪ Does it sometimes seem that there's always someone willing—even eager—to criticize you, to find fault with what you do, and to confidently predict that disaster will be the result of your actions? Such people seem eternally ready to dampen our enthusiasm by saying, "I told you so."

Even Jesus had critics waiting to stone him. Critics can make us feel guilty, ashamed, or just plain incompetent—if we let them. They're like porcupines in a balloon factory, poised to deflate us and take away any good feelings.

Stop listening to such critics. We all have areas that are vulnerable. When critics approach these areas, we go on red alert. Declare our soft spots off-limits. Say, "Don't tell me how to fix this problem. That's my business, not yours."

Let's start listening to nurturing voices, people who endorse our self-worth and cherish us as a holy, unrepeatable person fashioned in the image and likeness of God. Nurturing voices encourage us to believe that who we are today is not who we will be tomorrow. They remind us that we're always changing, learning, growing, and discovering. These people see in us a present-moment miracle, blessed with abundant possibilities.

Open your heart to hear God's gentle whisper: "Become who you are—special, beautiful, unique, terrific, lovable, and capable."

SERVE IT UP ▪ When we appreciate others, their value increases and our value increases. Show others that you appreciate them! Pick up that phone and tell nurturing people that you love them and let them know how much they mean to you.

PRAY IT UP ▪ *Jesus, may I always hear your voice affirming my dignity as a unique child of God. Amen.*

March 28 ✝ Saturday of the Fifth Week

EZEKIEL 37:21–28 • JOHN 11:45–56

Soaring Like an Eagle

Many of the Jews therefore, who...had seen what Jesus did, believed in him. **JOHN 11:45**

GIVE IT UP ▪ God challenges us to march to the beat of a different drum by not letting society squeeze us into its mold. There should be a recognizable difference between us and people who don't know God. We should talk differently. Have a different attitude. Live by a higher standard. Have the courage to be different.

But if I behave differently, my friends may make fun of me! Big deal! If I act like the good Christian I am, my friends may not want to hang around me anymore. Good! We don't need friends like that. The only thing standing between us and doing the right thing is the people with whom we choose to associate. Maybe it's time to make a clean break and ask God to bring us people who'll build us up and share our vision.

Be everything God created you to be by soaring above mediocrity to excellence. I once heard, "Don't be a thermometer that just measures the temperature; be a thermostat that changes the temperature."

Jesus did the right thing by searching out—and speaking up for—the forgotten, broken, and marginalized people who lived on the fringes of the crowd, even when it upset others. We soar when we refuse to ignore the soft cries of the shy and overlooked; when we feel the isolation and loneliness of the brokenhearted; when we speak up about injustices and endorse people's inalienable right to a life of value and dignity.

SERVE IT UP ▪ Commit yourself today to be different and to stop doing what everybody else is doing. Make a pledge to soar and never to ignore the one lost sheep or misplaced coin at home, at school, or at work.

PRAY IT UP ▪ *Jesus, when I look into the fringes of the crowd, at those pushed aside, and notice the eyes of pain, help me find you. Amen.*

MATTHEW 21:1–11 • ISAIAH 50:4–7 • PHILIPPIANS 2:6–11
MATTHEW 26:14—27:66 *or* 27:11–54

What a Week!

You will all become deserters because of me this night.... MATTHEW 26:31

GIVE IT UP ▪ George and Edna sat quietly in the hospital's family room. Their fifty-two-year-old son had recently been found dead, and the ER doctor asked me to tell them. After giving them the news, I discovered a younger son was on a heart transplant list and their daughter had bladder cancer. Edna looked me in the eye and said, "It's only Monday. What a week this is going to be!"

Jesus' week gets off to a good start with a hero's welcome—coats and palm branches spread in his path. *Messiah!* Several days later, their cheers turn to jeers. *Crucify him!* The crowds turn on him, saying this so-called messiah hadn't changed anything. *Crucify him!* But then again, they're just the crowd. Easily swayed. Not at all loyal. Not really friends.

Look closely at Jesus' "real friends." In a matter of hours, Jesus enjoys time with his disciples. He dips his hand in the same bowl with the man who'll betray him with a kiss. Jesus washes the feet of Peter, James, and John, who won't even stay awake to pray with him. In the courtyard, while he's being mistreated, he hears a rooster crow and turns to hear a beloved friend say, "I don't know him."

So what do we do when we too say, "What a week!"? Welcome these experiences, saying, "Jesus has been there and now Jesus is here to help me rebound!" Next, do something. Reach out to those who have already been there. Accept their support. Then embrace the next fifty-two weeks with enthusiasm, because we've still got plenty of living to do.

SERVE IT UP ▪ Pass out erasers to people having "What a week!" experiences. Remind them that Jesus will erase what's happened, slowly and gently.

PRAY IT UP ▪ *Jesus, help me see this week with renewed joy and help others do the same. Amen.*

ISAIAH 42:1–7 • JOHN 12:1–11

Do You Really Need It?

You always have the poor with you, but you do not always have me. JOHN 12:8

GIVE IT UP ▪ Billy is a little fish with big dreams. Leaving his family, he heads for the ocean to pursue the great life. He swims and swims, but can't find the ocean. Finally, he comes across Alfred, a wise old fish. "Can you tell me how to get to the ocean?" Alfred says, "Son, you're in the ocean." Billy replies, "But this is only water."

Jesus' mother, Mary, is a swimmer. She's living a life rooted in a never-take-for-granted relationship with others and a faith-filled relationship with Jesus, believing Jesus will nourish her soul by giving her all she needs. She's swimming in an ocean of gratitude and appreciation for who she has and what she has and could rightfully pray, "What more do I need?"

On the other hand, the apostle Judas is a searcher. He searches and schemes in a huge body of water. Desperate for more wealth and power, he floats past the important stuff. His insatiable attitude of "What's in it for me?" drowns him in waters of backstabbing and betrayal, and he's washed up on the shores of regret and remorse when it's too late.

Swimmers believe that prayer means being grateful for God's blessings in their lives; they ask only for what they need. They pay attention to what they have instead of being fixated on what they don't have.

Are you swimming in the ocean or searching for it?

SERVE IT UP ▪ Add a *blessing eggs-pression* this Easter. On a hard-boiled or plastic egg, each family member writes to the others, acknowledging how each is a blessing: "You bring joy into our lives!" "Thanks for listening!" Put them in each other's Easter baskets. Or, call a loved one to express your gratitude and praise.

PRAY IT UP ▪ *Jesus, I want to recognize the ocean of your love and fully appreciate it. Guide me along the way. Amen.*

ISAIAH 49:1–6 • JOHN 13:21–33, 36–38

Patient Healing

Very truly, I tell you, one of you will betray me. **JOHN 13:21**

GIVE IT UP ▪ I asked the members of Mending Hearts, a group that meets in our parish, how they feel when someone betrays them. They mentioned "a sick feeling," an inability to sleep, and a lack of trust.

Lisa compared trust to a bowl. Once broken, it can be repaired, but the cracks will be a part of the bowl forevermore. Others felt like their hearts were ripped out. Trust, dreams, and hope all shattered in an instant.

When people are betrayed, they go into a self-protective mode to ensure it won't happen again. It's a time of "grieving." From listening to my group, I've come up with this emotional process:

Response. "I can't believe this happened!"

Retreat. "Who needs people? They let you down."

Regret. "I should have listened to so-and-so."

Rage. "I'm so angry, I could...."

Revenge. "I'll get even someday."

Repair. "I want to be free from the pain."

Betrayal violates our faith in another person. Take your time grieving. Speak with a professional or join a group to help you move toward a healthy mindset.

SERVE IT UP ▪ Practice the 3 Ps with someone close who's been betrayed—patience, patience, and patience.

PRAY IT UP ▪ *Jesus, heal me slowly, but heal me. Amen.*

ISAIAH 50:4–9A • MATTHEW 26:14–25

Just Ask

What will you give me if I betray him to you? MATTHEW 26:15

GIVE IT UP ▪ Judas had no obvious vices. He had no dishonorable past like Matthew, the tax collector-turned-disciple. Peter was notorious for his impulsiveness, and James and John for their bad tempers. Yet nothing critical is said about Judas. He must have had an honest face and acted in a way that made him appear trustworthy. Still, Judas sold out a friend for thirty silver pieces and so is forever labeled as a betrayer. What motivated him to do so? Greed? Jealousy? Who knows? But we do know regret tormented his life enough that he ended it. During those darkest moments, Judas must have felt "unforgivable."

Folklore gives us many stories about Judas. One African legend tells about the moment Judas died. Before passing from this world to the next, he walked down a dark road and saw a house all lit up. Approaching it, he knocked on the door. Jesus opened it, embraced Judas, and invited him to come inside to eat.

It's a lifelong challenge to forgive those we feel don't deserve a second chance. But holding back on forgiveness builds an unscalable wall. When we move toward forgiveness, we give the person an opportunity to be healed. Imagine if Jesus withheld forgiveness as easily as we do. What would our list of unforgiven sins look like today? While Jesus' willingness to forgive doesn't give us license to deliberately mess up, we can ask for the wisdom to learn from the mess-ups—and the strength to stop repeating them.

SERVE IT UP ▪ Make little cards that say "Just ask" and pass them out to people who are having a hard time asking Jesus to forgive them. (Keep one for yourself as a reminder.)

PRAY IT UP ▪ *Jesus, when I bring my sins and mess-ups to you, you cast them into the sea and tell me no fishing is allowed. Thanks for the reminder. Amen.*

CHRISM MASS: ISAIAH 61:1–3A, 6A, 8B–9 • REVELATION 1:5–8 • LUKE 4:16–21

EVENING MASS OF THE LORD'S SUPPER: EXODUS 12:1–8, 11–14
1 CORINTHIANS 11:23–26 • JOHN 13:1–15

Leave the Latch Off

You also ought to wash one another's feet. JOHN 13:14

GIVE IT UP ▪ In the Russian Orthodox Church, there were people called *poustinikki* who devoted themselves to lives of prayer. They withdrew to the desert (*poustinia*) and lived in solitude, but not isolation. (The Russian word for solitude means "being with everybody.") By custom, the latch was always off the door as a sign of availability. The *poustinikki*'s priority was always a neighbor's need. We, too, are to live with the latch off the door to our hearts.

How have we helped the helpless, served the lonely, or rescued the despairing during Lent? Don't just stop at Lent. Here are some ideas for any time of year. Read a story to a blind person. Write a letter for someone crippled with arthritis. Pray the Rosary with nursing home residents. Rake yards, mow grass, or shovel snow for a neighbor who needs help. Plant flowers, clean up the pews after Mass, or babysit. Volunteer at a soup kitchen, a clothing or food pantry, or a local shelter. Check on a friend who's going through a difficult time. Small gestures say "I care about you."

Avoid the litany of excuses for leaving the latch on the door: "Sorry, no time," "If I'd only known, I would've helped," or "Why didn't you call me?" Keep alert for ways to help others. Leaving the latch off the door is their invitation to come inside and be refreshed. And when we walk forward on this holy night, we'll feel Jesus' gentle nudge to leave our churches and immerse ourselves in the lives of hurting, hungry people.

SERVE IT UP ▪ Be committed to reaching out in love to those in need. Do whatever it takes to lift someone's cross, and you'll have an exciting, rich, and meaningful life.

PRAY IT UP ▪ *Jesus, help me realize that when I wash others' feet, I may be washing yours. Amen.*

ISAIAH 52:13—53:12 • HEBREWS 4:14–16; 5:7–9 • JOHN 18:1—19:42

Let It Go

Then he bowed his head and gave up his spirit. JOHN 19:30

GIVE IT UP ▪ Are you holding on to past hurts? What you do with your hurt determines whether you live freely or in a prison of pain. What have you never gotten over? That time when you fell flat on your face and were embarrassed? Physical, emotional, or perhaps even sexual abuse? Maybe you still remember the constant ridicule from a parent. Perhaps you've had a failed marriage. What is it that—even now—brings the resentment back?

Jesus wants to set you free so you can get on with your life. Don't think about the past. Let it go. Jesus can relate to your hurt. Laughed at. Mocked. Beaten. Deserted by friends. Jesus knows all about being hurt. You'll never be free from your past until Jesus is in your life. You'll just keep reacting to things from the past. Things that keep you from moving into the present. Jesus stays close to the brokenhearted. He wants to comfort and help you.

When Jesus comes into your life, you don't have to clean up your house first. He doesn't say, "Get your act together and then come to me." He says, "Let me into your life, and I'll help you clean it up." Talk to Jesus. Listen to what he has to say. Then nail your hurts to his cross and let them die. What do you have to lose? The pain of your past hurts!

SERVE IT UP ▪ You think nobody understands what you've been through—and you may be right. But Jesus always understands. And he's somebody! If you're in pain today, say, "Jesus is with me."

Take a nail. Squeeze into it all the hurts and pains that keep popping up in your head. Then push the nail deep into the ground and forget where you buried it.

PRAY IT UP ▪ *Jesus, I need your help to let go of the past. Amen.*

EASTER VIGIL: GENESIS 1:1—2:2 *or* 1:1, 26–31A • GENESIS 22:1–18 *or* 22:1–2, 9A, 10–13, 15–18 • EXODUS 14:15—15:1 • ISAIAH 54:5–14 • ISAIAH 55:1–11 • BARUCH 3:9–15, 32—4:4 • EZEKIEL 36:16–17A, 18–28 • ROMANS 6:3–11 • MATTHEW 28:1–10

It's Never Too Late to Start Over

He is not here; for he has been raised, as he said. MATTHEW 28:6

GIVE IT UP ▪ One of the fascinating things about the Easter story is the sudden change in the disciples. One minute they're defeated, the next minute they're dynamic. One minute they're crushed, the next minute they're confident. One minute they're having a pity party, the next minute they're taking on the world. What made the difference?

Jesus—giving them the confidence to start over.

Have you ever been halfway through a project or a career and wanted to start over? Or halfway through your life and wanted to start over? Jesus says, "You can start over. I'm going to help you." Jesus wants to help you. That's the good news of Easter.

Jesus specializes in new beginnings. He wants to do something fresh in your life. That's what Easter is all about: starting over.

It's never too late to start over. God says, "There is hope! I don't care how low you go or where you've been." The message of Easter is that Jesus doesn't care where you've been or what your past has been. What matters is the direction of your feet right now. Where are you headed?

The good news of Easter is that Jesus rose from the dead. I know it's a cliché, but this Easter can be the first day of the rest of your life. Jesus Christ wants to give you the confidence to start over and to keep going.

SERVE IT UP ▪ Perhaps you know people who are barely hanging on. Their health is going down the tubes, or their marriages are disintegrating. Read the Easter story with them. Encourage them to begin again. Give them a packet of flower seeds to remind them of the possibilities for new growth and fresh starts.

PRAY IT UP ▪ *Jesus, you give me the power and confidence to pick myself up and start over. Thank you! Alleluia! Amen.*